Need to Know

abis

...y

www.heinemann.co.uk
visit our website to find out more information about **Heinemann Library** books.

To order:

☎ Phone 44 (0) 1865 888066

🖹 Send a fax to 44 (0) 1865 314091

🖥 Visit the Heinemann Bookshop at www.heinemann.co.uk to browse our catalogue and order online.

First published in Great Britain by Heinemann Library, Halley Court, Jordan Hill, Oxford OX2 8EJ,
part of Harcourt Education.

Heinemann is a registered trademark of Harcourt Education Ltd.

Designed by M2 Graphic Design
Originated by Ambassador Litho Ltd
Printed in China by South China Printers

ISBN 0431 09795X (hardback)   ISBN 0431 098026 (paperback)
06 05 04 03 02   07 06 05 04 03
10 9 8 7 6 5 4 3 2 1   10 9 8 7 6 5 4 3 2 1

British Library Cataloguing in Publication Data
Connolly, Sean,
Cannabis – (Need to know)
1.Cannabis – Juvenile literature 2.Cannabis – Physiological effect – Juvenile literature
3.Drug abuse – Juvenile literature
I Title
362.2' 95

Acknowledgements
The Publishers would like to thank the following for permission to reproduce photographs: Ancient Art and
Architecture Collection p18, Corbis pp6, 7 (Phil Schermeister), 21, 22, 23, 24, 26, 35, 42, 47, Corbis
Stock Market pp8, 49, David Hoffman pp30, 31, Getty Images p51, GettyOne p32, Imagebank pp41, 44,
Network p15, Photofusion pp12, 27, 29, Popperfotto pp13, 38, Rex Features pp17, 25, 39, Science Photo
Library pp5, 11, 37, 40, Stone pp28, 33, 45, Werner Forman p19.

Cover photographs reproduced with permission of Janine Wiedel Photo Library and Tudor Photography.

Every effort has been made to contact copyright holders of any material reproduced in this book. Any
omissions will be rectified in subsequent printings if notice is given to the Publishers.

Contents

Any words appearing in the text in bold, **like this**, are explained in the Glossary.

Cannabis

Cannabis is the most widely used illegal drug in the world. Like alcohol it has been around for thousands of years, but the Western world has only been exposed to it in large quantities for the last 50 years or so. Even in that relatively short period, cannabis use has grown rapidly. Its users come from all walks of life and represent nearly every age group.

Obvious questions

With so many people taking cannabis, society needs to know the answers to many questions about it – just what effects it has in the short term and over time. In a nutshell, the questions boil down to a single one: is cannabis dangerous? Scientists have been trying to answer this question for some time, and a number of things already seem clear. Cannabis, like any mind-altering drug, makes it hard for people to make accurate decisions – when driving, operating machinery or even walking near traffic. Smoking cannabis cigarettes is far more harmful than smoking tobacco because cannabis contains many more chemicals that damage the lungs.

Even more worrying are the **psychological** effects of taking cannabis, particularly over long periods. While **high**, people often feel moody and even begin to have horrible fears that the world is 'out to get them'. Over time, regular users can develop a need for the drug, usually described as psychological **dependence.** For these people, going without cannabis makes them irritable, restless and fearful. Even more worrying is the way that regular cannabis use seems to make people want to escape from reality, hiding behind the changed mood created by the high. Many regular cannabis users lose interest in making new friends and trying new hobbies or interests.

Understanding the law

Some people view cannabis as relatively harmless, and argue that it should be **decriminalized** – the legal penalties against it should be lessened. Others even say that it should be legalized – removing all penalties for having or selling it. However, cannabis remains illegal precisely because governments need to look after the interests of the people. They believe it is in the interest of the people not to be exposed to a drug that could do them harm – even if we are, as yet, unsure about the extent of that harm. It is hardly surprising that the medical world remains concerned about a drug of which the primary effect is to distort the way people think and feel.

Cannabis leaf is rolled, like tobacco, into cigarettes known as 'joints' or 'spliffs'.

What is cannabis?

Most people learn about cannabis by word of mouth, relying on hearsay and rumour to get a picture about the drug and its effects. This way of passing on information distorts the truth about cannabis, since inaccuracies become greater with each retelling. Also, since the person passing on the information is often trying to persuade someone else to try cannabis for the first time – or perhaps trying to sell it – there are often exaggerations and boastful claims about its effects or harmlessness.

The cannabis plant

The term cannabis, used throughout this book, refers to a group of mind-altering products that derive from a bushy plant that grows from 1–6 metres tall. There are three **species** of cannabis plants that produce mind-altering drugs: *Cannabis sativa*, *Cannabis indica* and *Cannabis ruderalis*. The *sativa* species has been grown for many centuries and is used to make a variety of useful products including rope, cloth and paper. Most of these goods are produced from hemp, a strong fibre that comes from the stem of the plant. It is the leaves and flowers of this plant, as well as the *indica* and *ruderalis* species, that are dried to produce **intoxicating** effects.

Cannabis usually grows in warm places that have a great deal of sunshine. Many of the 'source' countries for cannabis – including Colombia, Thailand and Nigeria – are places where it grows naturally and without any real need for cultivation. Also, because hemp was a valuable item in the 19th century – it was vital in the age of sailing ships – cannabis was widely cultivated across southern USA. Growing conditions there are favourable, and the plant has spread widely as a weed.

Cannabis users in Europe and North America are constantly trying to find new varieties that can grow in greenhouses or which have more **potency**. Some of these varieties, such as **skunk** (so named because of its distinctive foul smell) are several times stronger than ordinary cannabis.

Cannabis cultivation grew in the 19th-century 'golden age' of sailing, since the hemp was used to make ropes.

What is cannabis?

How it is taken

The dried leaves and flowers of the plant form the bulk of the illegal cannabis market around the world. People smoke this form of cannabis, either rolled in a cigarette that is often called a joint or in pipes, water pipes and 'bongs' (small water pipes). Some people mix the cannabis with tobacco when they roll a joint.

The other main product is **hashish**, which comes from the **resin** of the cannabis plant. This resin hardens and dealers sell it in a range of shapes, including sticky balls, chunks or flakes. Hashish is either smoked (again, often mixed with tobacco) or cooked, in cakes and biscuits, and eaten. Although already more than double the strength of ordinary cannabis, hashish can be boiled in a **solvent** such as alcohol to produce 'hash oil'. This hash oil is usually mixed with tobacco or leaf cannabis, but sometimes smoked on its own in a pipe. It is up to 25 times as **potent** as normal cannabis and creates a quicker and more powerful **high**. Since the high is strengthened, so too are the side effects of paranoia and unease that many people feel with cannabis.

Active ingredient

Cannabis is known as a **psychoactive** drug, meaning that it affects a person's thinking. The cannabis plant contains more than 400 different chemicals and several of these are psychoactive. The most important of these is delta-9-tetrahydrocannabinol (**THC**), which is present in the resin of the plant. Cannabis resin is concentrated in the buds of the plant, but it is also present in weaker concentrations in the leaves and stems.

The amount, or concentration, of THC in the cannabis determines its strength and the extent of the high. Ordinary cannabis, of the sort that is rolled and smoked, contains between 1 and 8 per cent THC. Hashish, made from the resin itself, can have THC concentrations of up to 14 per cent. Hash oil, which has had much of the non-THC material boiled away or filtered out, can have THC concentrations of 50 per cent or more.

Known by many names

Cannabis and the many products made from it are known by various common terms or nicknames. Some of the terms used to describe the dried leaves include 'marijuana', 'reefer', 'pot', 'herb', 'ganja', 'grass', 'old man', 'blanche', 'weed', 'bhang', 'dagga' and simply 'smoke'. Hashish is often shortened to 'hash' and sometimes referred to as 'tar'. Hash oil is sometimes known as 'oil'.

Most types of cannabis are smoked to allow the active ingredient, THC, to enter the bloodstream quickly.

How widespread is it?

Cannabis use around the world is widespread and studies indicate that its use is rising. It is by far the most commonly used illegal drug. In 2000, the European Monitoring Centre for Drugs and Drug Addiction published a report indicating that 45 million Europeans use cannabis regularly. A British survey, carried out around the same time, showed that one in ten people in England and Wales had used cannabis in the past year.

Detailed surveys carried out by Britain's Institute for the Study of Drug **Dependence** (ISDD) suggest that cannabis use hits its peak among the young. These surveys indicated that more than 1 in 3 people in the 16–19 year-old range (about 35 per cent) had taken cannabis at least once, about 30 per cent had taken it in the past year and 18 per cent had used it in the last month.

The Australian **Illicit** Drug Report of 2000 also showed that cannabis use among the young was widespread – and probably rising. Despite forming a National Illicit Drugs Strategy at a cost of A$295 million, Australia has seen illicit drug use actually rise in the past five years. Not all of this drug use is cannabis, of course, but the most recent studies indicate that 40 per cent of the population over 14 years of age have tried cannabis at least once.

The USA yo-yo

The figures for the USA echo most of these trends, but they also paint a fuller picture of how cannabis use has fluctuated over time. In 1998, 8.3 per cent of youths aged 12–17 were current users of cannabis. Over the past 20 years, however, use within this age group has changed. The figure for the 12–17 year-old group in the USA reached a peak of 14.2 per cent in 1979, declined to 3.4 per cent in 1992, more than doubled from 1992 to 1995 (8.2 per cent) and has gone up and down since then.

The 1999 National Household Survey on Drug Abuse (NHSDA) estimated that 5.1 per cent (11.2 million) of the population of the USA aged twelve and older were monthly marijuana or **hashish** users, which is the same rate as in 1991 – but considerably lower than the rate of 13.2 per cent in 1979. The NHSDA also found that the number of first-time cannabis users in 1998 (2.3 million) had increased significantly compared to 1989 (1.4 million).

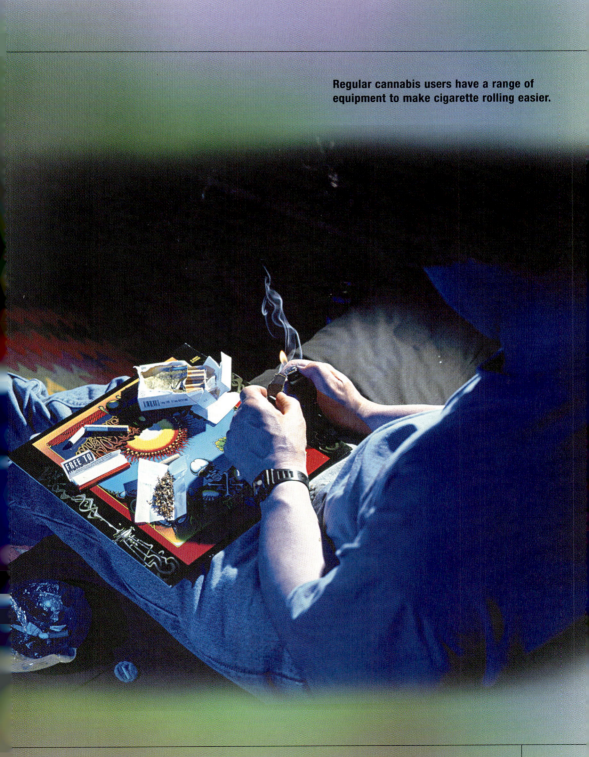

Regular cannabis users have a range of equipment to make cigarette rolling easier.

Voices of protest

Some people who are currently in positions of power and influence have become involved in campaigns to legalize cannabis, or at least to have it **decriminalized**. In some cases, these people have used the drug in the past and believe that it did them no harm. It is this view – that cannabis is basically harmless – that lies behind all their arguments. Legalizing cannabis would remove all legal controls against having or selling it. Cannabis would then be treated like alcohol or tobacco.

Decriminalizing cannabis would not go quite so far. It would still be considered illegal to sell and have large quantities, but people selling or possessing small amounts would not be arrested. They might have to pay a small fine, but there would be no permanent police record that they had committed a crime (as there is now).

These people believe that making cannabis legal – or almost legal – would help society in general. The police would be able to concentrate on 'more important' activities such as violent crime. The government would earn money from taxes paid on cannabis, and those who need cannabis for medical reasons (see pages 26–27) would have free access to supplies.

In the UK, the *Independent on Sunday* newspaper ran a series of articles in favour of decriminalization in 2000. The issue is even more publicized in the USA, with several national organizations leading efforts for changes in the cannabis laws. One of the leading groups is the National Organization for the Reform of Marijuana Laws (NORML).

People might use cannabis during all-night parties (left). Others who favour decriminalization (above) mount organized public demonstrations.

Is cannabis addictive?

Although the terms **addictive** and **addict** are often used in relation to drugs, most medical professionals prefer the terms 'dependent' and 'dependent user'. Part of the reason for this slight change of terms has to do with social matters: the word 'addictive' carries a sense of being uncontrollable and even unforgivable. 'Dependent', on the other hand, suggests a type of behaviour that can be overcome. Professionals also find it useful to talk of someone being either physically dependent or **psychologically** dependent on a drug.

A drug is said to cause physical **dependence** if the user continually needs to increase the dose to maintain the effects of the drug – a pattern called **tolerance** – and then suffers **withdrawal** symptoms when it is stopped. Alcohol and heroin are good examples of drugs that cause physical dependence. Psychological dependence is to do with the mind's 'need' for the drug to cope with stress or difficult situations. Alcohol also produces a psychological dependence, as do cocaine and amphetamines.

The case of cannabis

The question of whether cannabis produces dependence has been one of the main reasons why scientists have studied it so closely. Many of these studies have been organized or monitored by the National Institute on Drug Abuse (NIDA) in the USA. In a recent report, former NIDA director Dr Charles Schuster pointed out that regular cannabis use does produce dependence – both physical and psychological.

One of the main signs that someone is dependent on a drug is how they behave when they cannot have it. Dr Schuster found that many regular cannabis users stopped eating properly, became anxious and depressed, lost sleep and even began to shake when their supply was stopped suddenly. These are classic signs of withdrawal, a feature of physical dependence.

Psychologically, people also show a need to continue to use cannabis if they have become regular users. These users become sluggish and withdrawn, unwilling to make decisions or even to show much enthusiasm about anything. 'Younger users lose interest in school, sports and clubs,' says Dr Schuster. Their lives seem to narrow in focus as they concentrate simply on drug-taking.

Drug rehabilitation centres regularly deal with people who are concerned about their cannabis use.

Is cannabis addictive?

Evidence of the users

Most regular users would not publicly admit that they are **dependent** in any way on cannabis. It is part of the image of cannabis that people can cope, remaining 'cool' and detached from everyday cares. Sometimes this view is echoed by professionals. However, in private, many of these same regular users often tell a different story.

'A lot of people think it [cannabis] is not addictive,' says Ron Kadden of the University of Connecticut Health Center. 'Users have been told by treatment professionals and friends that they couldn't really be addicted to marijuana.' Kadden adds that many people contacted him when he advertised a treatment programme designed to tackle the problem of cannabis dependence. It was the users themselves who concluded that cannabis use led to dependence, and that they needed help.

The Dutch approach

The Dutch government, like other governments, is concerned about widespread drug use among the young. While they support medical efforts to identify how – and if – cannabis use leads to dependence, they also accept that it is difficult to stop supplies reaching people. So the Netherlands has chosen to try to isolate the use of cannabis in order to get people to cut down on its use.

Over the past three decades the Netherlands has adopted a tolerant approach to the use of 'soft' drugs such as cannabis. It has **decriminalized** possession below a certain amount and turned a blind eye to small-scale sales in Amsterdam's 'brown cafes' and elsewhere. The Dutch view this policy as a success, pointing out that hard drug dependence is falling and that the use of cannabis is actually less widespread than it is in Britain and in other countries where it remains illegal.

> **"It is important to note that these effects [of physical dependence] occur after only a few weeks of constant use and at dosages that would be common among street users."**
>
> (Dr Charles Schuster, former director of the National Institute on Drug Abuse)

The Dutch allow people to smoke limited amounts of cannabis in Amsterdam's 'brown cafes'.

The roots of the 'weed'

Cannabis cultivation and use go back thousands of years in human history, even if it has not been used to get **high** throughout that time. Scientists believe that the wild version of the *Cannabis sativa* plant originated in Central Asia. **Nomadic** people took the plant and its seeds and spread it further afield, especially in East and South Asia. In these settings, with heavy rainfall and long hours of sunshine, the cannabis plant thrived and grew in the wild. It is likely that at this time cannabis was seen mainly as a source of useful fibres, although the lack of written records from this period – more than 5000 years ago – leaves many gaps in our knowledge.

It is certain, though, that the Chinese soon recognized the strength and durability of the hemp fibres. They sowed seeds close together in order to produce long-stemmed plants. The hemp twines enabled the Chinese to produce strong fishing nets, stout ropes and hard-wearing mats. It is also from this time that the first recorded medical use of cannabis can be found. Cannabis is included in a list of medicines compiled for the Chinese Emperor Shen Nung around 2727 BC.

Spreading the 'cure'

During this period the Chinese were beginning to use other parts of the cannabis plant, besides the hemp-producing stems. They made cooking oil from the extracted seeds and this oil was also used as a herbal remedy for cramps and fever. News of the healing properties of cannabis spread into India some time after 2000 BC, and the plant was introduced by new settlers there at that time. The Indians used cannabis for a wide range of medical treatments – including curing constipation. They also believed that cannabis would reduce sexual urges. Holy men took cannabis for this purpose.

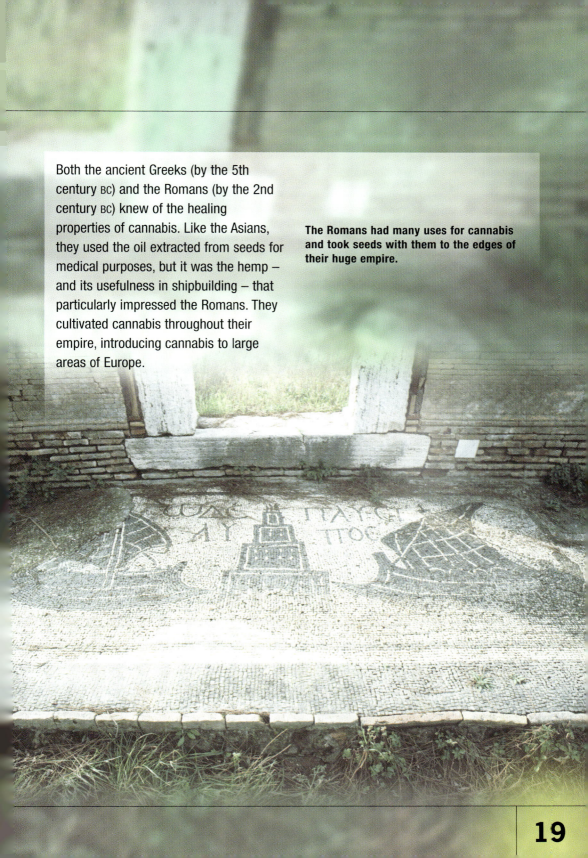

Both the ancient Greeks (by the 5th century BC) and the Romans (by the 2nd century BC) knew of the healing properties of cannabis. Like the Asians, they used the oil extracted from seeds for medical purposes, but it was the hemp – and its usefulness in shipbuilding – that particularly impressed the Romans. They cultivated cannabis throughout their empire, introducing cannabis to large areas of Europe.

The Romans had many uses for cannabis and took seeds with them to the edges of their huge empire.

Rampant growth

From about 1500 onwards, Europeans began to take more interest in cannabis. This was the beginning of the great age of exploration and maritime trade, so demand for hemp to make rope and canvas sails grew rapidly. The word 'canvas' is said to come from a Dutch pronunciation of the Greek word cannabis. At the same time, people began to look for different types of natural cures for illnesses. **Herbalists** re-examined ancient Greek and Roman medical records and began to spread the word about the properties of cannabis.

Rise and fall

One of the most famous 17th-century herbalists, Nicholas Culpepper of England, claimed that cannabis could be used to treat swellings, aches and pains, and even to combat **parasites**. European settlers took cannabis plants with them to the Americas, where the dual purpose of the plant – industrial and medical – continued to be appreciated. George Washington grew the plant at his Mount Vernon home. Historians looking at his diaries suggest that he set aside the potent female plants for his own medicinal use. Moreover, in the 18th and 19th centuries, people became more interested in science and technology. The **Scientific Revolution**, which spread through Europe and beyond in the 18th and 19th centuries, cast doubts on established folk remedies. Many herbal preparations (which are only now being rediscovered) were discredited and linked to medieval superstition.

Exotic influences

Although cannabis fell from favour as a medicinal aid in Europe, it remained commonly used in Asia and the Middle East. Arabs and Asians also continued to understand its mind-changing effects. Many European travellers to Arab lands – and especially soldiers in Napoleon's far-flung military campaigns – experimented with cannabis. They took the practice home with them. Beginning in France, cannabis (especially in the form of **hashish**) became popular among artists, writers and others who styled themselves as **bohemians**. By the 1850s the trend had gained momentum and the *Club des Haschischins* (Hashish-users Club) was formed in Paris. Its members included the great writers Dumas, Baudelaire, Flaubert and Balzac.

Gustave Flaubert (1821–80) was a French novelist and a member of the *Club des Haschischins*.

The modern scene

The roots of the modern use of cannabis – with users from most elements of society – can be traced to the arts, if not necessarily the *Club des Haschischins* and its European counterparts. Artists and writers in most societies used cannabis, but the real rise came with the constantly moving population within the USA. It was at the beginning of the 20th century that the USA really began to develop. New people arrived from around the world, looking for jobs. Americans themselves also began to move to new areas within their own large country. These 'newcomers', whether foreign or American-born, tended to move to cities, where many of them first came across cannabis.

Cannabis became even more popular among the city populations after the First World War (1914–18) because the government in the USA **outlawed** alcoholic drinks in a law known as **Prohibition**. Jazz musicians used cannabis regularly, and the authorities became concerned that this spreading use would lead to a crime wave – cannabis was linked to violence and criminal behaviour. In 1936 two respected magazines, *Popular Science Monthly* and *Scientific American*, published long pieces condemning cannabis as a menace to American society. By the end of the decade, every state in the USA had passed laws against its use.

Films such as the 1936 *Reefer Madness* painted a sometimes-exaggerated picture of the threat posed by cannabis.

Youth culture

Cannabis remained a hidden part of society in the USA, Britain, Australia and many other countries for several decades. The decades immediately after the Second World War (1939–45), however, saw the real boom in its use. Young people became more aware of drugs generally, and now they could afford them. Writers such as Jack Kerouac wrote of their experiences with cannabis in the 1950s and many young readers followed his example. By the early 1960s people were finding it easier to get hold of cannabis, and a new wave of rock musicians referred to it constantly in their songs.

Because cannabis was seen as a 'softer', less risky **high** than that of other drugs, it gained an unofficial acceptance among many people who would not consider using anything stronger. Since its breakthrough in the 1960s cannabis has remained a constant, retaining its popularity while other drugs – such as cocaine and ecstasy – capture the public eye for a while but come and go in and out of fashion.

Bob Marley, Jamaica's legendary reggae musician, was a regular user of cannabis.

Who takes cannabis?

Many drugs are associated with a particular group within society, who might be termed 'high risk' and at whom drug-awareness campaigns might be targeted. For example, a large proportion of heroin and crack cocaine users come from poor, inner-city environments. Anabolic steroids are linked to athletes and people who have hobbies involving muscle building and weight training. Cannabis, however, is different. Like alcohol and tobacco, it is used in such quantity that it is impossible to give a profile of a typical user. Nevertheless, there are some trends within its pattern of use.

Starting young

In common with alcohol and tobacco, cannabis attracts young people as first-time users. Teenage users remain the most frequent users of cannabis, a figure that seems to be common in most countries (see page 10).

Many of the factors that lead young people to try alcohol and tobacco are also at work with cannabis. One of the most important is peer pressure; the feeling that someone will be considered not 'cool' or daring if he or she does not try it. This pressure is tied in with the sense that most people's parents will not approve and the sense of daring increases because cannabis is not just frowned upon, but it is illegal. Just as a young drinker or smoker has probably never met someone who lost a job because of **alcoholism** or developed lung cancer because of smoking, a young cannabis user is unlikely to meet former users who felt that their lives had become worse because of cannabis.

Unspoken approval?

Of course, young people are not the only people who use cannabis. Many older people, who perhaps first used cannabis in their teens, continue to smoke the occasional joint or turn a blind eye if someone else does at a party. Young people pick up on these signals and interpret them as a 'green light' to use cannabis themselves. When it becomes apparent that people with power and influence are trying to change society's ideas about cannabis (see page 12), the signals that a young person can receive become very mixed.

> **"They used to show off at school – the boys mostly. 'I had draw [cannabis] last night, I was well buzzing' – lots of showing off."**
>
> **(Lisa, aged 18, quoted in *Drugs Wise*)**

Young people begin using cannabis early in a setting where adults are regular smokers themselves.

Medicinal uses

One of the most important – and hotly debated – issues surrounding cannabis is whether it has any real medical benefit. Any drug that can be proved to reduce pain, or make life easier for ailing patients is welcomed by society. In the case of cannabis, though, the position becomes trickier because many of those who want it legalized for **recreational** use believe that the first step is to persuade people that it is beneficial to health. As a result, studies that do make this suggestion are sometimes seen as being part of the pro-cannabis campaign, rather than **impartial** scientific work.

Some pro-cannabis campaigners argue that cannabis can lessen the pain and nausea that many people experience in chemotherapy.

Long history

Up until around 1900, cannabis was used widely to stimulate the appetite, to relax muscles and to combat pain. From that point on, though, this use declined because other drugs became widely available. Any further medical research stopped in the 1930s; the Marijuana Tax Act of 1937 in the USA was the most important **legislation** to curb any more study of cannabis.

With the increased use of cannabis in the 1960s, stories began circulating about how cannabis users were gaining relief from a number of medical conditions. Three of the most common conditions mentioned were glaucoma (an eye illness), multiple sclerosis (which affects the muscles) and the nausea produced by

chemotherapy treatment against cancer. In the case of the first two, cannabis seemed to reduce pressure in the eyes and muscular stiffness. Because even the medical use of cannabis is severely limited, or even illegal, it is hard for medical science to make a definitive judgement on how effective cannabis (or **THC**) really is.

Keeping it illegal

Not everyone is convinced, however, that widening the availability of cannabis via medical use is a good idea. The California Narcotics Officers' Association, a fierce opponent of liberalizing cannabis laws, makes this position quite clear:

'Common sense dictates that it is not good medical practice to allow a substance to be used as a medicine if that product is:

- not Federal Drugs Agency (FDA) approved
- made up of hundreds of different chemicals
- not subject to product liability regulations
- exempt from quality control standards
- not governed by recommended daily doses
- offered in unknown strengths (THC) from 1 to 10+ per cent
- taken by the patient himself or herself.'

Many multiple sclerosis patients say that cannabis relaxes muscles that have become stiff as a result of this disease.

The effects of cannabis

Like so many other aspects of cannabis, the experience and sensations that it produces are varied and hard to describe fully. Many cannabis users do not even feel any different – and certainly not 'stoned' or **high** – the first few times that they try it. Even for those who take cannabis regularly, the effects can vary according to the person's mood or depending on the strength and type of the cannabis itself.

Laid back

People take cannabis in order to achieve a sense of relaxation – the comfortable feeling that is often described as being laid back. It begins a few minutes after smoking the cannabis. Coupled with this sense of relaxation is a heightening of the senses: sights, sounds and tastes seem to become more vivid. Something that the person might normally find slightly funny becomes hilarious when the person is high.

This sense of relaxation also plays tricks with concentration, short-term memory and the person's sense of time. People who are high often begin long sentences, only to forget how the sentence was meant to end. The passage of time seems to be slowed, and people sometimes use the term 'pot time' to describe the way brief events seemed to stretch on and on. The high lasts for two to three hours, near the end of which people often become suddenly hungry (this feeling is termed the 'munchies').

Unpleasant shocks

Some people feel an acute sense of anxiety after they have smoked cannabis. Sometimes this unsettling feeling occurs even after the first puff, and it can border on **paranoia**. It is at this point that people believe that everyone is looking at them, judging them and talking about them when they are looking away.

The sensation known as the 'munchies' leaves cannabis users craving a quick food fix, often in the form of a late-night takeaway.

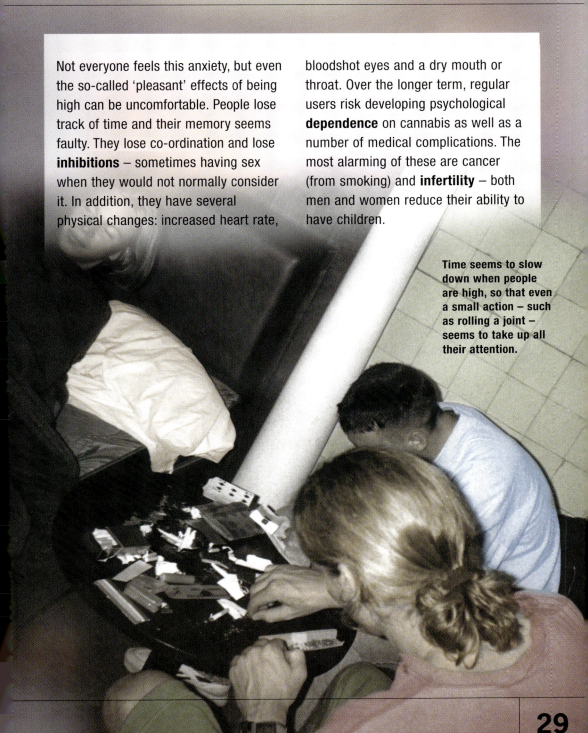

Not everyone feels this anxiety, but even the so-called 'pleasant' effects of being high can be uncomfortable. People lose track of time and their memory seems faulty. They lose co-ordination and lose **inhibitions** – sometimes having sex when they would not normally consider it. In addition, they have several physical changes: increased heart rate, bloodshot eyes and a dry mouth or throat. Over the longer term, regular users risk developing psychological **dependence** on cannabis as well as a number of medical complications. The most alarming of these are cancer (from smoking) and **infertility** – both men and women reduce their ability to have children.

Time seems to slow down when people are high, so that even a small action – such as rolling a joint – seems to take up all their attention.

How does cannabis work?

Cannabis takes effect when its active chemical ingredient, **THC**, reaches the brain. How much THC reaches the brain – and how long it takes to get there – depends mainly on how the person has taken the cannabis and also on the **potency** (percentage of THC) of the cannabis itself. Most people smoke cannabis, where the rich supply of blood in the lungs absorbs THC. Blood from the lungs goes first to the heart and then to the brain, so the **high** – as well as some other side effects – can occur within minutes. These side effects include increased heart rate and blood pressure, and the tell-tale bloodshot eyes of the user.

Eating cannabis produces the same effects, but the process takes longer because the blood has longer to travel; also, the liver breaks down some of the THC along the way. The high, as well as the side effects, develop more slowly and can take up to 90 minutes.

Inside the brain

Once it has reached the brain, the THC forms **chemical bonds** with special **receptors** using **compounds** that are already present in the brain. Alcohol and heroin work in a similar way, at least in terms of bonding with receptors in the brain. The receptors that deal with THC are located in the *hippocampus*; the region of the brain that is crucially involved in the formation of new memories. This fact is significant because one of the most common negative side effects of cannabis – both short-term and long-term – concerns memory loss and inability to hold on to recently acquired knowledge.

The rush of THC into the brain is achieved quickly when cannabis is smoked from a water pipe.

Craving more?

Cannabis also bonds with receptors in other parts of the brain, in regions that deal with co-ordination and fine movement (other areas that are often affected during a high). The brain stem (which regulates breathing), however, remains unaffected which means that it is impossible to suffer a fatal overdose of cannabis. The most dramatic, and as yet not fully conclusive, evidence concerns **dopamines**. Scientists know that heroin, certain other drugs (including alcohol) and even some foods release a 'messenger' called dopamine that rushes a 'pleasure message' through the brain. The brain remembers the pleasure and works to repeat it. Recent experiments dealing with THC indicate that the drug might also activate dopamine. If so, then it would prove that cannabis leads to **dependence**.

Cannabis smoking becomes a way of life for some users, as one joint leads to another. The brain equates the drug with pleasure, and 'programs' the body to take in more.

Getting hold of cannabis

One of the reasons underlying the widespread use of cannabis is how easy it is to get hold of supplies. Before the 1970s, most cannabis used in the USA, the UK and Australia was imported. Most of the supplies in the USA came overland from South and Central America and through Mexico. North African and Asian supplies went to European and Australian markets. All of these trade routes still exist, although the 'home-grown' industry in most consumer countries also accounts for a rising proportion of cannabis that is sold.

Making the deal

In the UK, people might pay £100 or more for an ounce of cannabis in leaf form. Resin sells for about £60–100 for an ounce, the higher price reflecting the greater amount of THC. Prices rise and fall according to available supplies, and if there is a shortage (perhaps caused by a large police seizure of imported cannabis) the price increases. Home-grown cannabis, which plays an

increasing role in the overall market (partly because there is less risk of being caught by customs officials), has kept prices more or less level for more than a decade. As imported supplies dry up temporarily, home-produced supplies fill the gap and hold the price steady.

Because there is so much cannabis around, coming from various suppliers, the arrangements for buying and selling it are less rigid than those governing the sale of cocaine, LSD, heroin or other drugs. Some dealers sell only cannabis because they draw a distinction between it and other, more obviously harmful, drugs.

Cannabis, in leaf form, is usually sold in air-tight bags.

Targeting youth

This loose network means that cannabis is relatively easy to buy. Despite the zero tolerance approach of many school systems in the USA, many targeted buyers are school age. First-time users of cannabis are often in secondary school or the equivalent. A 1998 study by the US National Center on Addiction and Substance Abuse indicates that adolescents are first exposed to, and try, cannabis at a very young age. According to the study, 50 per cent of 13-year-olds reported that they could find and purchase cannabis, and 49 per cent of teens surveyed said that they first tried it at the age of 13 or even younger.

Cannabis deals are usually made in pubs and clubs where young people gather.

The cannabis industry

The traditional cannabis industry was based on production in certain regions (South and Central America, North Africa and South-East Asia) and exports into consumer countries in Europe, North America and Australia. Because most forms of cannabis (apart from resin) take up a great deal of space, comparatively little is smuggled into countries in aircraft luggage. Instead, importers use trucks and ships to move supplies around. Overland routes into Britain have used Spain and the Netherlands as 'gateways'. Boats carrying cannabis to Britain and Australia avoid busy shipping lanes and head for more remote coastal waters, where the cannabis is off-loaded at night on to smaller boats. The amounts of money involved in all this trade are enormous: the European cannabis trade alone is said to be worth about £7.5 billion a year.

Drug trafficking organizations operating from Mexico are responsible for supplying most of the foreign cannabis available in the USA. Virtually all cannabis is smuggled into the USA concealed in false compartments, fuel tanks, seats and tyres of private and commercial vehicles. Larger shipments are usually smuggled in tractor-trailer trucks in false compartments and among everyday bulk shipments, such as agricultural products. With increased law enforcement pressure along the south-west border of the USA, cannabis smugglers are shifting to traditional routes in the Gulf of Mexico and the Bahamas. They use cargo vessels, pleasure boats and fishing boats to sail up the coast of Mexico, either to USA ports or drop-off sites along the USA coast and the Bahamas.

Home-grown and new varieties

Cannabis grows like a weed in countries with warm, sunny climates. It needs little fertilizer in these conditions, and prolonged sunshine produces **THC**-rich buds. It is not surprising that many cannabis users in California, Australia and South Africa are able to grow their own supplies. These constitute the cheapest, and most easily produced, home grown cannabis. In certain areas – notably remote parts of California – home-grown cannabis far exceeds the amounts needed for the personal use of the growers. A substantial **black economy** has grown up in these regions, so that they become 'exporters' to parts of the country with less favourable growing conditions.

US customs officials, shown here along the Mexican borders, are constantly on the alert for large-scale shipments of cannabis into the country.

The cannabis industry

To stop the spread of cannabis cultivation, the USA's Drug Enforcement Agency (DEA) launched the Domestic Cannabis Eradication and Suppression Program in 1979; it is the only programme in the USA aimed solely at cannabis. It began operations in Hawaii and California, and rapidly expanded to include all 50 states of the USA by 1985.

Unlike vast wooded areas where cannabis plots could go virtually undetected, Northern Europe is densely populated and lacks such protective forest cover. Moreover, the unsettled climate would not suit wide-scale cultivation of cannabis. As a result, it is in the interest of this European home-grown (and greenhouse-dependent) sector to produce the highest-grade cannabis in the smallest area.

The Dutch, who are famous for their gardening skills, have taken advantage of their country's relatively liberal cannabis laws. Dutch growers have led the way in producing many high-**potency** strains in greenhouses. Some Dutch companies openly advertise cannabis seeds for sale and export, boasting about award-winning strains. **Skunk**, the high-concentration cannabis that gets its nickname because of its distinctive strong smell, is one such variety.

With the success of DEA efforts to root out cannabis plantations, many cannabis growers in the USA are moving indoors. Following the similar Dutch example, they have begun growing new strains that are stronger and can be harvested all year-round. The average **THC** content of US-produced *sinsemilla* (female cannabis) rose from 3.2 per cent in 1977, to 12.8 per cent in 1997. Indoor 'grows' range from several plants grown in a cupboard or wardrobe, to thousands of plants grown in elaborate, specially constructed greenhouses. In 1998, the five leading states for indoor growing activity were California, Florida, Oregon, Alaska and Kentucky.

Home-grown cannabis thrives with basic care – growers buy and sell seeds for potent strains.

Against liberalization

In the USA, many groups argue that any relaxation of the firm laws and attitudes towards cannabis should be resisted.

'It is our firm belief that any movement that liberalizes or legalizes substance abuse laws would set us back to the days of the 1970s when we experienced this country's worst drug problem and the subsequent consequences. In the 1980s, through the combined and concerted efforts of law enforcement, prevention and treatment professionals, illicit drug use was reduced by 50 per cent. Teenagers graduating from the class of 1992 had a 50 per cent less likely chance of using drugs than those who graduated in the class of 1979.'

(California Narcotic Officers' Association position paper)

❝ An Australian study in 1999 estimated that the market for cannabis was worth more than A$5 billion – more than twice the amount spent on wine.❞

Legal matters

In the UK, at the time of writing, cannabis is classified as a Class C drug. Police can issue someone caught in possession of it with either a formal warning or a formal caution. Both of these are put on police files – the warning is recorded locally and the caution goes on a national police record. Having a warning or caution on these records can affect future offences. Depending on the amount found – or whether the person has either a warning or caution already – the police can then charge that person. The maximum penalty for possession is two years in prison and/or a fine. For intent to supply, it is five years in prison and/or a fine.

Local laws

Penalties in both the USA and Australia are decided by the states themselves and can vary greatly. The penalty for possessing a small amount of cannabis in Texas, for example, is up to 180 days in prison and/or a fine of US$2000. Sentences and fines increase with the amount found and can reach 99 years in prison and a fine of US$50,000. Texan law is even harsher on those who sell, especially to young people. If someone is selling cannabis within 1000 feet (300m) of a school or 300 feet (90m) of a youth centre, public pool or video arcade: the penalty (already up to 99 years and US$100,000) doubles.

In South Australia, Australian Capital Territory and Northern Territory, minor possession and growing offences have been **decriminalized**, that is, offenders pay a fine and no conviction is recorded. In Victoria, first-time minor cannabis offenders are cautioned and referred to a drug education service. Federal law (enforced in customs cases, for example) is much harsher. Anyone arriving in Australia with 100 grams of cannabis is liable to new penalties of A$250,000 or 10 years' imprisonment.

Zero tolerance

States in the USA have a great deal of independence in deciding on laws governing the possession and sale of cannabis, but local school authorities are able to impose far stricter controls on pupils. Since the 1990s, most schools in the USA have adopted a policy of 'zero tolerance', which immediately penalizes (usually through expulsion) pupils for serious offences. Possession and sale of cannabis is one of these serious offences. For example, Texan schools operate their policy of zero tolerance under the guidance of a state law known as the 'Safe Schools Chapter'. Its wording is clear: 'Students who sell, give, deliver, possess, use or are under the influence of drugs, alcoholic beverages or abusable chemicals must be expelled.'

Customs officials target cargo ships (left) in their hunt for cannabis, but the police often swoop on individuals (below) to make their arrests.

Life with cannabis

Deception plays a large part in the lives of most drug users, and the same holds true with those who are regularly involved with cannabis. Many cannabis users believe that their behaviour is harmless. They point to the poor health and reduced mental performance of those who are 'hooked' on heroin or **dependent** on alcohol. As a result, they conclude that cannabis has none of those ill-effects. The truth is more complicated and more serious.

Being **high** on cannabis does affect someone's decision-making ability and this change can have profound consequences. For example, someone who is high might have the same reflex speed as usual when driving, but he or she could well have difficulty concentrating on the road. The same holds true with any activity that combines physical co-ordination with concentration, and the results could be deadly.

Effects in the longer term

Smoking anything over a long period increases a person's risk of suffering from **respiratory** diseases, including lung cancer. Prolonged cannabis use also almost certainly leads to changes in a person's character and behaviour, although it remains difficult to measure these changes. True scientific experiments (which can produce such conclusions) rely on a 'control', or a subject who does not take, for example, a drug while someone else does. There is no way that someone can lead two lives at the same time – one using cannabis regularly and the other not taking it – so the conclusions are based on what is called **anecdotal** evidence. This evidence, however, is consistent and persuasive.

The tricks cannabis plays on the mind make driving a dangerous proposition for anyone who is high.

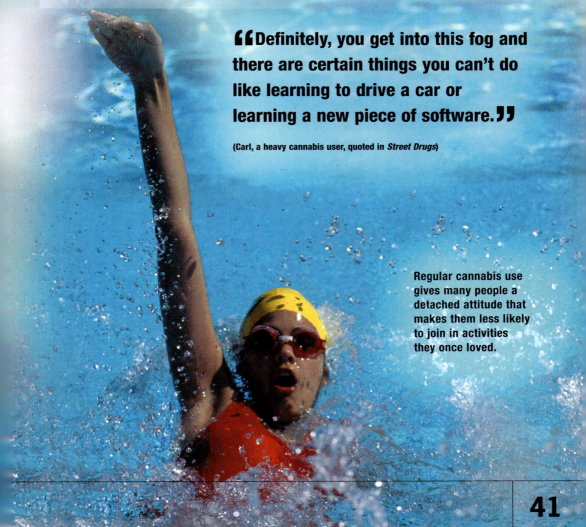

Some people argue that the disruption of the memory (which certainly occurs when someone is high) can become permanent. This is hard to prove, but a more general conclusion does seem to hold – that prolonged cannabis use can **demotivate** people. Becoming temporarily laid-back is one thing, but to throw away educational or career opportunities is far more serious. Drugs counsellors are very concerned that teenagers, whose futures depend on educational performance and important decisions, are damaging their own future prospects because of their 'so what' attitude towards such concerns.

"Definitely, you get into this fog and there are certain things you can't do like learning to drive a car or learning a new piece of software."

(Carl, a heavy cannabis user, quoted in *Street Drugs*)

Regular cannabis use gives many people a detached attitude that makes them less likely to join in activities they once loved.

Life with cannabis

'Missed the boat'

Greg, in his mid-thirties, is a part-time decorator who lives in a fishing village in the state of Maine in the USA. He believes that heavy cannabis use changed his life profoundly. 'I worked hard in high school and through college and was really pleased when I was accepted at a good law school. I had smoked joints from time to time with friends but when I found out that courses in law school were pass-fail and not graded I felt that I could put my feet up a bit and enjoy life. I started smoking more dope and missing classes; everything seemed OK because I was still passing the courses.

Life with cannabis often means just that – very little interests the user apart from the cannabis itself.

'I didn't know many of the lecturers but that didn't seem to matter. It turns out it did. I guess it was pretty obvious what I was up to and these guys [the academic staff at the law school] weren't exactly pleased that one of their students was so obviously unmotivated – plus doing something illegal! In my final year I was hauled into the dean's office and expelled: they quoted some obscure regulation and didn't mention dope outright, but I didn't need to read between the lines. It was hard trying to explain all this to my parents, but my father was really ill and my mother was too worried about him to react much.

'That was about fifteen years ago. You could say I sort of dropped out after that, living at home, still smoking dope and doing odd jobs. Most of my friends are married now but I feel I've kind of missed the boat.'

Genuine need?

In June 1999, the UK's Townswomen's Guild (which is not normally associated with civil protests) held their Annual General Meeting in the Royal Albert Hall in London. One of the prominent speakers was Clare Hodges from the Alliance for Cannabis Therapeutics. 'I've had multiple sclerosis for seventeen years and after I'd had it for ten years I began to find that I was getting very ill and I was getting no relief from the medicines,' she said. 'Somebody told me about cannabis, and I tried it – I was at my wit's end.'

Having listened to Ms Hodges' personal testimony, the Guild voted overwhelmingly in favour of legalizing cannabis for medicinal purposes. They were also swayed by the testimony of several doctors who reported that cannabis provided the only relief for patients suffering from chronic pain, bladder problems and who had difficulty in controlling muscle spasms. Both doctors and patients risk criminal prosecution for using cannabis and two patients have already been prosecuted for growing their own supplies.

"Everything in this world was created for a purpose, but people sometimes choose to abuse what God has given us. Marijuana is an example of this. Though used for purposes other than what it was created, it can and should be used for the medicinal purposes for which I'm sure God put it here."

(Katherine Haynie, a US respondent to a BBC on-line poll 'Should cannabis be legalized for medicinal use?')

Family and friends

Some cannabis users smoke an occasional joint, perhaps over a weekend, and feel that they are still very much in control of their lives. They believe this because the signs of being **high** are less obvious than, for example, being drunk. This often makes them think that they have fooled other members of their family.

Drifting along

Although the signs of being stoned as a one-off can be masked, it is less easy for a person to hide the fact that they are using cannabis regularly. Patterns of behaviour do change, along with a fundamental change of attitude.

The sense of being laid back, which for many people is one of the attractions of the cannabis high, carries over into everyday life. Things that once seemed important, such as studying hard, can appear absurd and many regular cannabis users look down on others who are caught up with the 'rat race' (as they see it) of competition and hard work. Many users get high before, during and after school, lying to their parents about what they are doing.

Family dinner can seem like a waste of time for someone who smokes cannabis regularly.

These changes in behaviour also affect friendships. Regular users usually find themselves in the company of fellow users, and grow apart from old friends. Quite apart from the changes of attitude in the regular users there is another big barrier: they are engaged in an illegal activity while their former friends are not. That barrier puts pressure on the friends, who often feel that they would be scorned if they informed to parents or teachers – even if they knew they were acting in the true spirit of friendship.

Cannabis users have a reputation for being aimless and unlikely to get excited about new activities.

❝I had never lived with the fear that I had no friends, so I did almost anything to keep the two good friends I still had. One of the things I did was try pot for the first time. This was a big change from the way I lived when I was younger. I was an athlete, and the last thing I thought I would get into was drugs. Drugs prevented me from being the best athlete I could be.❞

(Former user's account on the Marijuana Anonymous website)

Treatment and counselling

When people talk about treatment and counselling, they are usually referring to the large group of drugs that lead to **dependence**, especially physical dependence. Some form of outside help – in the form of therapy sessions, substitute drugs or one-on-one counselling – is often necessary to overcome the compulsive desire to have more of the drug. Cannabis is different. Dependence is hard to prove conclusively, although many users and former users believe that it is a definite problem. This uncertainty, ironically, can make it harder for cannabis users to face up to their problem than those who are hooked on heroin or who are problem drinkers – since both of these drugs are well-known examples of dependence drugs.

Coming off

Regular users often deny that they have a problem, even if they spend most of their time thinking about getting **high** or getting hold of supplies – if they aren't high already. Many believe those who argue that cannabis does not produce any type of dependence, physical or psychological, and this belief prevents them from seeing what effect cannabis is having on their lives.

Unlike most other drugs, including alcohol, **THC** (the active chemical in cannabis) is stored in the fat cells and therefore takes longer to clear the body than with any other common drug. This means that some parts of the body still retain THC even after a couple of months, rather than just the couple of days or weeks for water soluble drugs. During this time many people experience **psychological** or emotional symptoms such as **insomnia** and depression. Then, because THC tends to dampen the dreaming mechanism in the brain, vivid – and often disturbing – dreams return. Throughout this time users can feel at the mercy of their emotions, jumping from irritation and anger to **euphoria** and back again.

Although cannabis can never match the unsettling effects of coming off heroin (cold turkey) or alcohol (**delirium tremens** and the 'shakes'), many people do have physical symptoms. The most common are headaches and night sweats (sweating is one of the body's natural ways of getting rid of toxins). Many people also find that they lose their appetite for a few weeks, possibly losing weight or feeling nauseous as well. Most of these symptoms, like the psychological symptoms, are gone after two or three months.

Tackling dependence

Despite the voices that argue that cannabis does not lead to either psychological or physical dependence, many drug therapists believe that it is difficult for a regular user to cut down or stop. Many people do find that cannabis has become too important in their lives. One organization, Marijuana Anonymous (MA), offers a chance for such users to confront their own lives in a supportive atmosphere. MA is one of many organizations that model itself on Alcoholics Anonymous (AA), which has helped thousands of people overcome their dependence on alcohol.

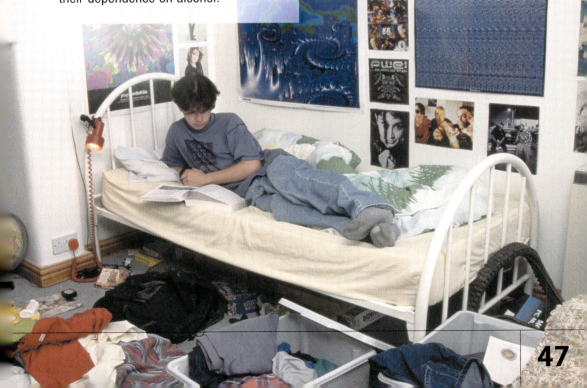

The real world can seem pale and dull without cannabis – especially if the former user lost interest in other activities during their time using the drug.

Treatment and counselling

Following the example set by AA, Marijuana Anonymous uses the same methods (comradeship, honesty and **anonymity** in meetings) and aims (to remain free of the substance).

MA asks regular cannabis users to consider its twelve questions (see right). A 'yes' answer to one or more of these questions can indicate a serious problem with cannabis. By acknowledging the problems themselves, cannabis users have taken the first (and hardest) step towards recovery. Shared experiences with other members provide a network of support and allows users to recognize that they are not alone.

"An informed citizenry... is the most effective deterrent of all."

(American Medical Association)

The twelve Marijuana Anonymous questions

1. Has smoking pot stopped being fun?
2. Do you ever get **high** alone?
3. Is it hard for you to imagine a life without marijuana?
4. Do you find that your friends are determined by your marijuana use?
5. Do you smoke marijuana to avoid dealing with your problems?
6. Do you smoke pot to cope with your feelings?
7. Does your marijuana use let you live in a privately defined world?
8. Have you ever failed to keep promises you made about cutting down or controlling your dope smoking?
9. Has your use of marijuana caused problems with memory, concentration, or motivation?
10. When your stash is nearly empty, do you feel anxious or worried about how to get more?
11. Do you plan your life around your marijuana use?
12. Have friends or relatives ever complained that your pot smoking is damaging your relationship with them?

Experienced counsellors have a lot to offer young people who might only have a confused idea about cannabis and its effects.

People to talk to

Although cannabis use has increased dramatically over the years, the information about it can still seem incomplete and contradictory to many young people. Some of the certainties about cannabis – such as the fact that you can get a criminal record for using it, get expelled from school or develop lung cancer in the longer term – can get distorted by word of mouth. Young people usually hear of the 'buzz' of the **high**, the giggles and the munchies – and never of the lethargy and lack of motivation among those who use cannabis over long periods. This type of peer pressure is not helpful, but it is a strong and persuasive force.

Other voices

There are, however, people who can put things in a different perspective, either by giving first-hand accounts of their own drug experiences or by outlining the clear dangers of any drug abuse. Parents and older family members are usually the best people to turn to first. In many cases, the parents of teenagers will have had first-hand exposure to cannabis themselves in their own youth. Nevertheless, the teenage years are often the period when young people feel that they have least in common with their parents. Even sympathetic teachers and others in authority locally might seem 'too close to home'.

The UK has a wide range of telephone contacts – many of them toll-free and most of them anonymous – where young people can find out more about cannabis and other drugs. Many of the organizations listed in the Information and advice section (pages 52–53) are specialist phone lines. They provide such a telephone service, or they can suggest local agencies throughout the UK. Others are geared specifically to queries coming from younger people. Whether you approach one of these organizations, a family member, a youth leader or teacher, the important thing is to be able to talk – and listen – freely about your drug concerns. Sharing a problem or worry is the first step to solving it.

Emotions are often heightened when a person is high – which is bad news if the emotion was fear or worry to begin with.

"This first major sign of success has occurred because parents, teachers, coaches, ministers and community coalitions, are all working together in a comprehensive national and local effort. The future should show additional improvements as well. The fact that the numbers are best for the youngest (12–17) group is a harbinger that use will continue to fall as this group grows older.**"**

(White House National Drug Policy Director Barry McCaffrey, referring to the drop in teenage cannabis use in the late 1990s)

Information and advice

The UK is well served by organizations providing advice, counselling and other information relating to drug use. All of the contacts listed on these pages are helpful springboards for obtaining such advice, or for providing confidential information over the telephone or by post.

Contacts in the UK

ADFAM NATIONAL, Waterbridge House, 32–36 Loman Street, London SE1 0EE Tel: 020 7928 8900
This is a national (UK) hotline for the friends and families of drug users. It provides confidential support and information to anyone who is worried about someone close to them using drugs.

British Association for Counselling (BAC) 1 Regent Place, Rugby CV21 2PJ
The BAC has an extensive directory of counselling services relating to drugs and other issues throughout the UK. Enquiries are by post only. Enclose a SAE for a list of counsellors in your area.

Drugscope, Waterbridge House, 32–36 Loman Street, London SE1 0EE, Tel: 020 7928 1211
Drugscope has the largest drug reference library in Europe and provides leaflets and other publications.

Narcotics Anonymous, PO Box 198J Tel: 0171 498 9904
Narcotics Anonymous (NA) is a network of self-help groups tackling the problem of drug **dependence** on the same lines as those of Alcoholics Anonymous.

National Drugs Helpline Tel: 0800 776600
The Helpline provides a toll-free telephone contact for all aspects of drug use and has a database covering all of the British Isles for further information about specific drugs or regional information.

Release, The National Drug and Legal Helpline, 388 Old Street, London EC1V 9LT, Tel: 020 7603 8654
Release operates a 24-hour helpline that provides advice on drug use and legal issues surrounding the subject.

Youth Access 1A Taylors Yard, 67 Alderbrook Road, London SW12 8AD, Tel: 020 8772 9900
Youth Access is an organization that refers young people to their local counselling service. It has a database of approximately 350 such services throughout the UK.

Contacts in the USA

Child Welfare League of America 440 First Street N.W., Washington, DC 20001, Tel: (202) 638-2952
The Child Welfare League of America, based in Washington, provides useful contacts across the country in most areas relating to young people's problems, many of them related to drug involvement.

D.A.R.E. America PO Box 775, Dumfries, VA 22026 Tel: (703) 860-3273
Drug Abuse Resistance and Education (D.A.R.E.) America is a national organization that links law-enforcement and educational resources to provide up-to-date and comprehensive information about all aspects of drug use.

Marijuana Anonymous
web site: www.marijuana-anonymous.org
The MA web site is a starting point for information on the organization's aims and activities, as well as comprehensive links to local branches of MA around the world.

Youth Power
300 Lakeside Drive, Oakland, CA 94612
Tel: (510) 451-6666, ext. 24
Youth Power is a nationwide (USA) organization involved in widening awareness of drug-related problems. It sponsors clubs and local affiliates across the country in an effort to help young people make their own sensible choices about drugs, and to work against the negative effects of peer pressure.

Contacts in Australia

ADCA
PO Box 269, Woden, ACT 2606
web site: www.adca.org.au
The Alcohol and other Drugs Council of Australia (ADCA), based in the Capital Territory, gives an overview of drug awareness organizations in Australia. Most of their work is carried out over the Internet but the postal address provides a useful link for those who are not online.

Australian Drug Foundation
409 King Street, West Melbourne,
VIC 3003, Tel: 03 9278 8100
The Australian Drug Foundation (ADF) has a wide range of information on all aspects of drugs, their effects and the legal position in Australia. It also provides handy links to state and local-based drug organizations.

Centre for Education and Information on Drugs and Alcohol
Drug Programs Bureau, Level 3,
73 Miller Street, North Sydney
NSW 2059, Tel: 02 9391 9000
The Centre for Education and Information on Drugs and Alcohol is the ideal contact for information on drug programmes throughout Australia. It also has one of the most extensive libraries on drug-related subjects in the world.

Further reading

Buzzed, by Cynthia Kuhn, Scott Swartzwelder and Wilkie Wilson. W.W. Norton and Company, 1998.

Drugs, by Anita Naik. Part of Wise Guides Series. Hodder Children's Books, 1997.

Drugs and the Party Line, by Kevin Williamson. Canongate Books, 2001.

Drugs: The Facts, HEA leaflet. Health Education Authority, 1997.

Drugs Wise, by Melanie McFadyean. Icon books, 1997.

Learn to say no: Cannabis, by Angela Royston. Heinemann Library, 2000.

Street Drugs, by Andrew Tyler. Hodder and Stoughton, 2nd edition, 1995.

Taking Drugs Seriously, A Parent's Guide to Young People's Drug Use, by Julian Cohen and James Kay. Thorsons, 1994.

The Score: Facts about Drugs, HEA leaflet. Health Education Authority, 1998.

Glossary

addict
someone who is dependent on a drug

addictive
leading to dependence, as with a drug

alcoholism
disease linked to a dependence on alcohol

anecdotal
relying on descriptions rather than scientific experiments

anonymity
ability to keep one's name secret

black economy
illegal sale of products such as drugs; sometimes called the black market

bohemian
not worried about the rules set down by a society

chemical bonds
strong forces that bind atoms and molecules together

chemotherapy
cancer treatment that involves giving the patient a series of strong chemicals, but which leads to side effects such as fatigue and nausea

compound
substance that is composed of two or more elements

decriminalize
to eliminate criminal penalties or remove legal restrictions against something

delirium tremens
series of nightmare-like images and shaking that occurs when someone who is dependent on alcohol goes without it

demotivate
to cause someone to lose interest in things

dependence
need or craving for a substance, especially a drug. Can be either a psychological or a physical craving.

dopamine
chemical substance in the brain that regulates movement and emotion

drug trafficking
taking large amounts of drugs from one country to another illegally

euphoria
sense of profound happiness and well-being

hashish
often shortened to hash; a strong type of cannabis which comes from the resin of the cannabis plant

herbalist
someone who grows and understands the medicinal qualities of herbs

high
(in this sense) effect people feel after taking cannabis

illicit
against the law, illegal

impartial
fair and just, not biased

infertility
inability to have children because of medical problems

inhibition
sense of caution that stops people from behaving recklessly

insomnia
inability to fall asleep or remain asleep

intoxicating
causing someone to lose physical or mental control temporarily

legislation
laws based on acts passed by a representative body such as a parliament or congress

nomadic
constantly moving about, with no permanent home

outlaw
to make illegal

paranoia
belief that everyone is 'out to get you'

parasite
tiny creature such as an insect or worm that lives inside another animal

potency
strength of a chemical or drug

Prohibition
period (1919–1933) in the USA when alcoholic drinks were illegal

psychoactive
having an effect on the mind

psychological
dealing with the mind or brain

receptors
(in the human brain) organs that receive signals from the nervous system

recreational
(in terms of drugs) for pleasure, rather than as a medicine

resin
thick liquid containing the highest amounts of THC of any part of the cannabis plant

respiratory
relating to the lungs or breathing

Scientific Revolution
period in Europe, roughly from the late 1600s to the mid 1800s, when increased scientific curiosity led to many new discoveries

skunk
nickname of a particularly powerful variety of the cannabis plant

solvent
liquid that can dissolve many other substances, including chemicals that affect the human brain

species
scientific category of plants or animals. Individuals of the same species resemble each other and can only breed with others of the same species.

THC
delta-9-tetrahydrocannabinol, the active chemical ingredient of cannabis

tolerance
ability of the body to absorb increasing amounts of a drug

withdrawal
difficult process of giving up a drug, and the physical and psychological effects the process creates

Index